Cross Stitch Gifts
FOR CHILDREN

Dorothea Hall

☐MARK
PUBLISHING
5400 SCOTTS VALLEY DR.
SCOTTS VALLEY, CA 95066

Published 1992 by Merehurst Limited
Ferry House, 51-57 Lacy Road, Putney, London SW15 1PR
© Copyright 1992 Merehurst Limited

ISBN 0-937769-30-4

Distributed in the United States by
Mark Publishing, Inc.
5400 Scotts Valley Drive, Scotts Valley, CA 95066

Edited by Diana Brinton
Designed by Maggie Aldred
Photography by Di Lewis
Illustrations by John Hutchinson
Typesetting by BMD Graphics, Hemel Hempstead
Colour separation by Fotographics Limited, UK – Hong Kong
Printed in Hong Kong by Wing King Tong

*Merehurst is the leading publisher of craft books and has an excellent range
of titles to suit all levels. Please send to the address above for our
free catalogue, stating the title of this book.*

SUPPLIERS

The following mail order
company has supplied
some of the basic items
needed for making up the
projects in this book:

Framecraft Miniatures Limited
148-150 High Street
Aston
Birmingham, B6 4US
England
Telephone (021) 359 4442

*Addresses for Framecraft
worldwide*
Ireland Needlecraft Pty. Ltd.
2-4 Keppel Drive
Hallam, Victoria 3803
Australia

Danish Art Needlework
PO Box 442, Lethbridge
Alberta T1J 3Z1
Canada

Sanyei Imports
PO Box 5, Hashima Shi
Gifu 501-62
Japan

The Embroidery Shop
286 Queen Street
Masterton
New Zealand

Anne Brinkley Designs Inc.
246 Walnut Street
Newton
Mass. 02160
USA

S A Threads and Cottons Ltd.
43 Somerset Road
Cape Town
South Africa

For information on your
nearest stockist of
embroidery cotton,
contact the following:

DMC

USA
The DMC Corporation
Port Kearney Bld.
10 South Kearney
N.J. 07032-0650
Telephone: 201 589 0606

COATS AND ANCHOR

USA
Coats & Clark
P.O. Box 27067
Dept CO1
Greenville
SC 29616
Telephone: 803 234 0103

MADEIRA

U.S.A.
Madeira Marketing Limited
600 East 9th Street
Michigan City
IN 46360
Telephone: 219 873 1000

CONTENTS

Introduction   4
Basic Skills   4
Baby Hand-Toys   8
Teddy Bear Companions   12
Patchwork Quilt   20
Scatter Cushions   24
With Love and Kisses   32
Frilled Baby Basket   36
Miniature Pictures   40
Tied-On Pillow Cover   44
Conversion Chart   48
Acknowledgements   48

INTRODUCTION

Many people find the combination of cross stitch embroidery, with its tantalizingly varied effects, and projects for children quite irresistible. Who could fail to enjoy the simplicity of the animals cross stitched on the Baby Hand Toys, for example, or the single-coloured Patchwork Quilt for a doll's cradle, or the 'Three Bears' design on the Child's Chair Back and Cushion?

Children will love them! – and as cross stitch is genuinely one of the easiest stitches to master, they may wish to attempt the simpler projects. With a little adult help, this should be perfectly feasible – beginning, perhaps, with one of the hand toys.

Each cross stitch design is carefully charted and has an accompanying colour key and full instructions for making up the project. In addition, there is a Basic Skills section, which covers everything from how to prepare your fabric and stretch it in an embroidery frame to mounting your cross stitch ready for display.

Some of the designs, such as the hand toys and the doll's cradle quilt, are very easy to embroider and are eminently suitable for beginners. Others are a little more challenging, using several colours for shaded effects, and will be of interest to people with a little more experience, or those who are keen to widen their scope. Whatever your skills and interests, you will enjoy being able to create items from a wide range of projects, suitable for boys and girls of all ages.

BASIC SKILLS

BEFORE YOU BEGIN

PREPARING THE FABRIC

Even with an average amount of handling, many evenweave fabrics tend to fray at the edges, so it is a good idea to overcast the raw edges, using ordinary sewing thread, before you begin.

THE INSTRUCTIONS

Each project begins with a full list of the materials that you will require; Aida, Tula, Lugana and Linda are all fabrics produced by Zweigart. Note that the measurements given for the embroidery fabric include a minimum of 3cm (1¼in) all around to allow for stretching it in a frame and preparing the edges to prevent them from fraying.

A colour key for DMC stranded embroidery cotton is given with each chart. It is assumed that you will need to buy one skein of each colour mentioned, even though you may use less, but where two or more skeins are needed, this information is included in the main list of requirements.

Should you wish to use Coats/Anchor, or Madeira, stranded embroidery cottons, refer to the conversion chart given at the back of the book (page 48).

To work from the charts, particularly those where several symbols are used in close proximity, some readers may find it helpful to have the chart enlarged so that the squares and symbols can be seen more easily. Many photocopying services will do this for a minimum charge.

Before you begin to embroider, always mark the centre of the design with two lines of basting stitches, one vertical and one horizontal, running from edge to edge of the fabric, as indicated by the arrows on the charts.

As you stitch, use the centre lines given on the chart and the basting threads on your fabric as reference points for counting the squares and threads to position your design accurately.

WORKING IN A HOOP

A hoop is the most popular frame for use with small areas of embroidery. It consists of two rings, one fitted inside the other; the outer ring usually has an

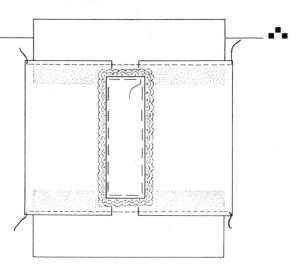

adjustable screw attachment so that it can be tightened to hold the stretched fabric in place. Hoops are available in several sizes, ranging from 10cm (4in) in diameter to quilting hoops with a diameter of 38cm (15in). Hoops with table stands or floor stands attached are also available.

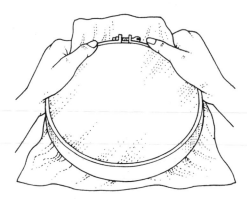

1 To stretch your fabric in a hoop, place the area to be embroidered over the inner ring and press the outer ring over it with the tension screw released. Tissue paper can be placed between the outer ring and the embroidery, so that the hoop does not mark the fabric. Lay the tissue paper over the fabric when you set it in the hoop, then tear away the central, embroidery area.

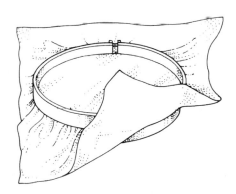

2 Smooth the fabric and, if needed, straighten the grain before tightening the screw. The fabric should be evenly stretched.

EXTENDING EMBROIDERY FABRIC
It is easy to extend a piece of embroidery fabric, such as a bookmark, to stretch it in a hoop.

● Fabric oddments of a similar weight can be used. Simply cut four pieces to size (in other words, to the measurement that will fit both the embroidery fabric and your hoop) and baste them to each side

of the embroidery fabric before stretching it in the hoop in the usual way.

WORKING IN A RECTANGULAR FRAME
Rectangular frames are more suitable for larger pieces of embroidery. They consist of two rollers, with tapes attached, and two flat side pieces, which slot into the rollers and are held in place by pegs or screw attachments. Available in different sizes, either alone or with adjustable table or floor stands, frames are measured by the length of the roller tape, and range in size from 30cm (12in) to 68cm (27in).

As alternatives to a slate frame, canvas stretchers and the backs of old picture frames can be used. Provided there is sufficient extra fabric around the finished size of the embroidery, the edges can be turned under and simply attached with drawing pins (thumb tacks) or staples.

1 To stretch your fabric in a rectangular frame, cut out the fabric, allowing at least an extra 5cm (2in) all around the finished size of the embroidery. Baste a single 12mm (½in) turning on the top and bottom edges and oversew strong tape, 2.5cm (1in) wide, to the other two sides. Mark the centre line both ways with basting stitches. Working from the centre outwards and using strong thread, oversew the top and bottom edges to the roller tapes. Fit the side pieces into the slots, and roll any extra fabric on one roller until the fabric is taut.

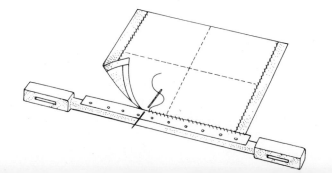

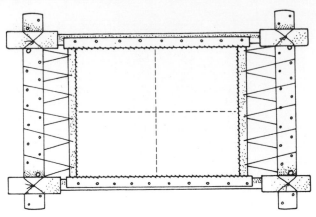

2 Insert the pegs or adjust the screw attachments to secure the frame. Thread a large-eyed needle (chenille needle) with strong thread or fine string and lace both edges, securing the ends around the intersections of the frame. Lace the webbing at 2.5cm (1in) intervals, stretching the fabric evenly.

ENLARGING A GRAPH PATTERN

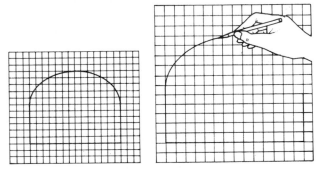

● To enlarge a graph pattern, you will need a sheet of graph paper ruled in 1cm (⅜in) squares, a ruler and pencil. If, for example, the scale is one square to 5cm (2in) you should first mark the appropriate lines to give a grid of the correct size. Copy the graph freehand from the small grid to the larger one, completing one square at a time. Use a ruler to draw the straight lines first, and then copy the freehand curves.

TO BIND AN EDGE

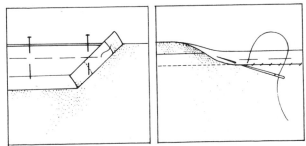

1 Open out the turning on one edge of the bias binding and pin in position on the right side of the fabric, matching the fold to the seamline. Fold over the cut end of the binding. Finish by overlapping the starting point by about 12mm (½in). Baste and machine stitch along the seamline.

2 Fold the binding over the raw edge to the wrong side, baste and, using matching sewing thread, neatly hem to finish.

PIPED SEAMS

Contrasting piping adds a special decorative finish to a seam and looks particularly attractive on items such as cushions and cosies.

You can cover piping cord with either bias-cut fabric of your choice or a bias binding; alternatively, ready-covered piping cord is available in several widths and many colours.

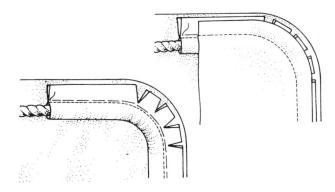

1 To apply piping, pin and baste it to the right side of the fabric, with seam lines matching. Clip into the seam allowance where necessary.

2 With right sides together, place the second piece of fabric on top, enclosing the piping. Baste and then either hand stitch in place or machine stitch, using a zipper foot. Stitch as close to the piping as possible, covering the first line of stitching.

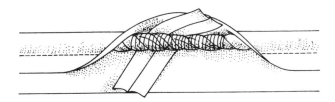

3 To join ends of piping cord together, first overlap the two ends by about 2.5cm (1in). Unpick the two cut ends of bias to reveal the cord. Join the bias strip as shown. Trim and press the seam open. Unravel and splice the two ends of the cord. Fold the bias strip over it, and finish basting around the edge.

MOUNTING EMBROIDERY

The cardboard should be cut to the size of the finished embroidery, with an extra 6mm (¼in) added all around to allow for the recess in the frame.

LIGHTWEIGHT FABRICS

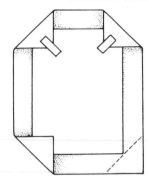 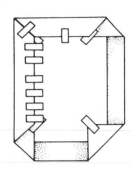

1 Place the emboidery face down, with the cardboard centred on top, and basting and pencil lines matching. Begin by folding over the fabric at each corner and securing it with masking tape.

2 Working first on one side and then the other, fold over the fabric on all sides and secure it firmly with pieces of masking tape, placed about 2.5cm (1in) apart. Also neaten the mitred corners with masking tape, pulling the fabric tightly to give a firm, smooth finish.

HEAVIER FABRICS

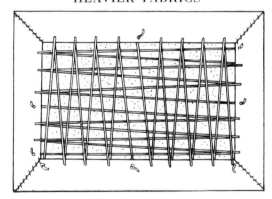

● Lay the embroidery face down, with the cardboard centred on top; fold over the edges of the fabric on opposite sides, making mitred folds at the corners, and lace across, using strong thread. Repeat on the other two sides. Finally, pull up the stitches fairly tightly to stretch the fabric firmly over the cardboard. Overstitch the mitred corners.

CROSS STITCH

For all cross stitch embroidery, the following two methods of working are used. In each case, neat rows of vertical stitches are produced on the back of the fabric.

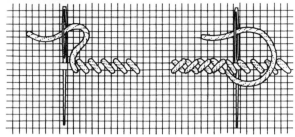

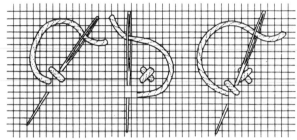

● When stitching large areas, work in horizontal rows. Working from right to left, complete the first row of evenly spaced diagonal stitches over the number of threads specified in the project instructions. Then, working from left to right, repeat the process. Continue in this way, making sure each stitch crosses in the same direction.

● When stitching diagonal lines, work downwards, completing each stitch before moving to the next.

BACKSTITCH

Backstitch is used in the projects to give emphasis to a particular foldline, an outline or a shadow. The stitches are worked over the same number of threads as the cross stitch, forming continuous straight or diagonal lines.

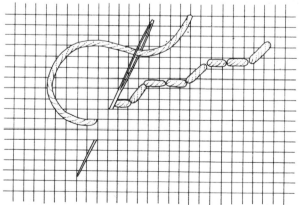

● Make the first stitch from left to right; pass the needle behind the fabric, and bring it out one stitch length ahead to the left. Repeat and continue in this way along the line.

Baby Hand-toys

Nursery animals, just big enough for
small hands to hold, are embroidered
on one side only in colourful cross
stitch patterns.
These easy-to-sew shapes are gently
padded to give roundness and
softness, and when a toy is not being
held by baby, it can be hung at the
side of the crib by its ribbon loop.

BABY HAND-TOYS

YOU WILL NEED

For three Hand toys, each measuring approximately 13cm × 9cm (5in × 3½in):

Six 18cm × 13cm (7¼in × 5in) rectangles of white Hardanger, 22 threads to 2.5cm (1in); two pieces for each toy
DMC stranded embroidery cotton in the colours given in the panels
Sufficient loose synthetic filling for each toy
90cm (1yd) of white satin ribbon, 6mm (¼in) wide
No26 tapestry needle
Matching sewing thread
Three 15cm × 10cm (6in × 4in) pieces of cardboard (use a breakfast cereal box, or similar packaging)
Tracing paper

THE EMBROIDERY

All three toys are embroidered and made up in the same way. For each toy, prepare one of the two pieces of evenweave fabric and stretch it in a frame, see page 5. Following the appropriate chart, complete the cross stitching, using two strands of thread in the needle throughout, and working one cross stitch over two threads of ground fabric. Steam press on the wrong side, if needed.

MAKING UP THE TOYS

Trace the outline of the appropriate toy; transfer it to the cardboard, marking the position of the arrows. Cut out the template; centre it on the wrong side of the embroidery, matching the edges of the cross stitching and aligning the arrows. Draw round the shape with a pencil.

Working freehand, draw a second (cutting) line 6mm (¼in) beyond the first pencil (stitching) line. Do not cut out the toy shape at this stage; the fabric tends to fray during sewing, and it is therefore best to complete the stitching first.

Cut the ribbon into three equal lengths; set two aside for the remaining toys, and fold one length in

half. Place the back and embroidered front fabrics right sides together. With the cut ends of the ribbon protruding just beyond the raw edges of the fabric, lay the folded ribbon between the two sections, as marked on the chart.

With the ribbon inside, pin and baste the sections together, stitching between the two marked lines. Using matching sewing thread, either machine stitch or backstitch around the edge, sewing on the seamline and leaving a small opening for the filling, as indicated on the chart.

Cut out, following the outer pencil line. Snip into any curves, taking care not to cut the seam. Remove the basting stitches and turn the toy through to the right side. Steam press, and then finger press the seam flat.

Gently fill the toy, using a knitting needle to push small amounts of the filling into awkward shapes, such as the cat's ears. Turn in the edges of the opening and slipstitch to close.

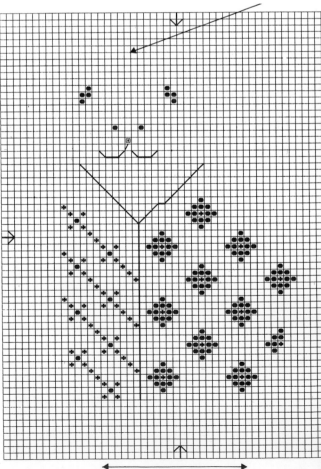

Attach ribbon

Leave open

Attach ribbon

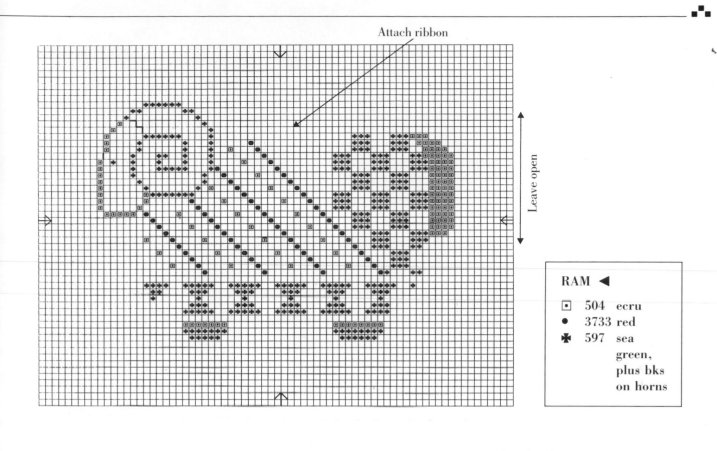

Leave open

RAM ◀

⊡ 504 ecru
● 3733 red
✽ 597 sea
       green,
       plus bks
       on horns

Attach ribbon

TEDDY ▶

⊡ 744 yellow
● 833 ochre, plus
       bks nose
       and mouth
✽ 581 olive green,
       plus bks
       shirt and
       trousers

CAT ◀

✽ 3705 red
● 334 light blue
⊡ 798 deep blue,
       plus bks
       mouth and
       body

Leave open

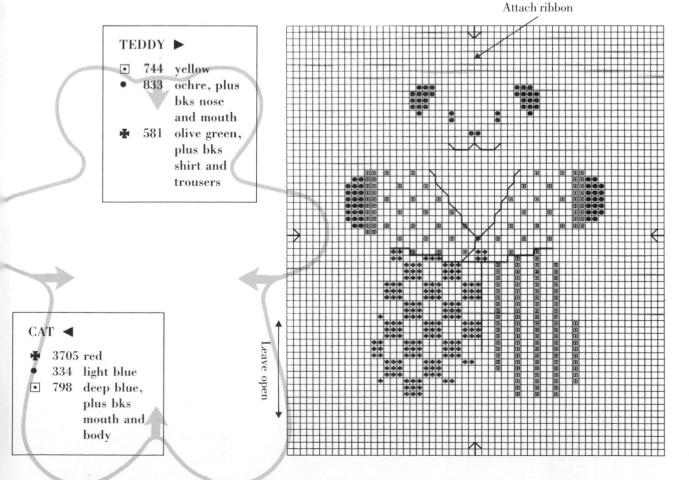

Teddy Bear Companions

The story of the Three Bears is the
perfect choice for decorating a
cushion and padded back for a child's
chair. The ingenious tie-on back
incorporates a deep pocket,
sufficiently large to hold a child's
favourite possessions, including
several cuddly toys.

If you wish to economize on the
evenweave fabric, you could make the
cushion back and the back pocket of
the tie-on back from plain or
patterned furnishing or other
heavyweight cotton. Note, however,
that the padded front portion is made
from one piece, folded over.

TEDDY BEAR COMPANIONS

YOU WILL NEED

For a chair back measuring 23cm × 20cm
(9in × 8in), and a chair cushion measuring
23cm (9in) square, excluding the frills,
which are 4cm (1½in) wide:

*60cm (⅔yd) of pale khaki evenweave Aida fabric,
110cm (43in) wide, 16 threads to 2.5cm (1in)
30cm (12in) of matching cotton sateen,
90cm (36in) wide, for the frills
120cm (1⅓yd) of contrasting seam binding,
12mm (½in) wide
24cm × 23cm (9½in × 9in) of medium-weight
synthetic batting
DMC stranded embroidery cotton in the colours
given in the panels
No26 tapestry needle
25cm (10in) square cushion pad*

PREPARING THE FABRIC

Following the cutting layout, cut out the chair-back
and the cushion sections from evenweave fabric.
Seam allowances are included in the measurements
given in the diagram.

Cut the sateen fabric into three strips across,
each measuring 10cm (4in) deep, and put these to
one side.

THE EMBROIDERY

Both the chair-back and the cushion are embroidered in the same way. With the fabric prepared
and stretched in a frame (see page 5), centre lines
basted in both directions and position line marked
for the chair-back design (Back 2), begin the cross
stitching.

Working with two strands of thread in the needle
and following the appropriate chart, complete the
embroidery. Work the backstitching last of all and
note that a single strand is used for the lines on the
rush seat of the chair-back design. Remove the
finished embroidery from the frame and steam press
it on the wrong side.

CUTTING LAYOUT

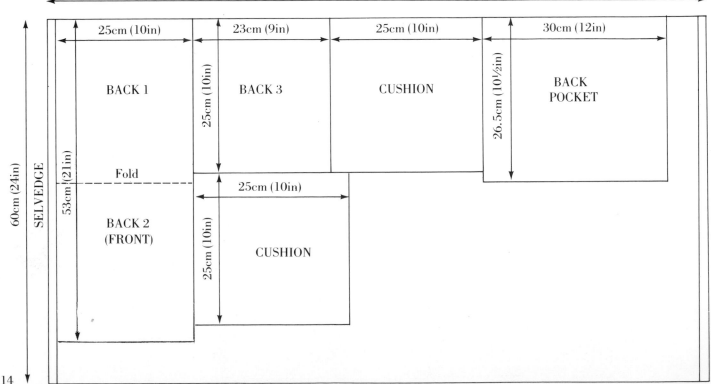

MAKING UP THE CHAIR-BACK

Using the basting lines as a guide, trim the fabric to measure 48.5cm × 23cm (19in × 9in), making sure the embroidered motif stays in the centre of the front section.

To make the frill, cut two 50cm (20in) lengths of sateen. Fold each piece lengthwise in half, right sides together, and machine stitch along the short edges. Turn through and press. Run a gathering thread along the bottom edge of each frill and pull up to measure 23cm (9in). With the right side facing, baste the frill to each long side of the front section raw edges just inside the seam allowance. Machine stitch in place.

For the ties, cut the seam binding into four equal lengths. Baste to the two short edges as shown in the diagram, so that the binding lies on the right side of the fabric and will be attached as the seams are sewn.

Place the batting on the wrong side of the lining section (Back 3), with the raw edges of three sides matching, and pin and baste it in position. Fold a single 12mm (½in) turning, enclosing the batting, at the remaining (chair top) edge of the back lining, and baste. With right sides together and the folded edge at the top (centre foldline), place the lining on the embroidered section. Stitch along the side and bottom edges. Trim the batting back and trim across the corners, then turn right side out and machine close to the fold along the top edge, stitching through all layers.

On the pocket section, machine stitch a double 12mm (½in) turning on one long edge. Make a pleat 2cm (¾in) deep at each side of the bottom edge, 6cm (2½in) in from the outer edge, and baste across.

On the main section, snip into the seam allowance on the foldline. Place the pocket section with the right side facing the wrong side of Back 1. Baste and machine stitch around three sides, leaving the top unstitched. Trim the corners and turn through to the right side. Machine stitch across the corners of the pocket top to strengthen.

MAKING UP THE CUSHION

To make the frill, join together the remaining lengths of sateen along the short edges to give a total length of 186cm (63in). Machine stitch the two

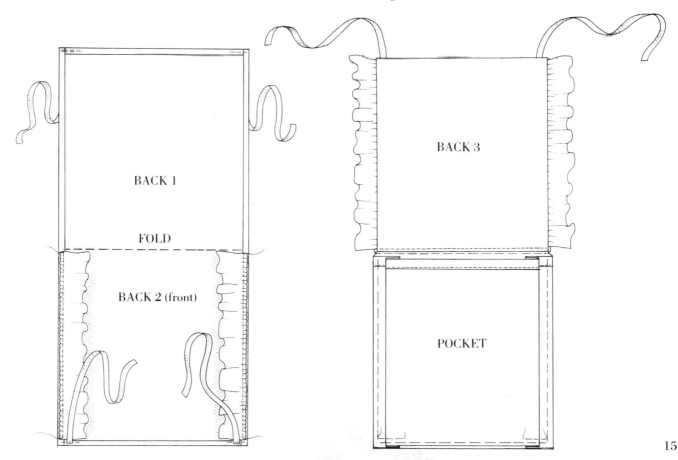

BACK 1

FOLD

BACK 2 (front)

BACK 3

POCKET

short edges together to form a circle, then turn through to the right side and press the seam open.

Fold the circular piece lengthwise in half, with wrong sides together, and press the fold. Run a gathering thread through both thicknesses along the lower edge and pull up the gathers to fit. Pin and baste to the right side of the cushion front, and stitch as for the chair-back.

Place the backing fabric and the embroidery right sides together, then baste and machine stitch around, leaving a 15cm (6in) opening in the middle of one side. Trim across the corners and turn through to the right side. Remove the basting threads and lightly press. Insert the cushion pad and slipstitch the opening to close.

To protect the finished embroidery from scuff marks and other accidents, it would be a good idea to spray it with a proprietory dirt repellant.

CUSHION ▼

‖	white	△	783 deep gold	Ι	807 turquoise	⊡	435 light brown
⊖	3047 cream	◆	224 pale pink	÷	598 blue		(bks 3781)
∽	676 pale yellow	●	3733 pink	↓	523 drab green	○	611 brown (bks 3781)
	(bks claws)	◣	504 pale turquoise		(bks on tablecloth)	✱	3781 dark brown
			(bks 733)	△	733 green	=	453 grey

CHAIR BACK ▲

◺	white	◆	224 pale pink	✲	435 light brown
S	3047 cream (bks 783)	⊡	3733 pink (bks 504)		(horizontal bks on
I	676 pale yellow	◣	504 pale turquoise		chair front)
△	783 deep gold (bks 3781)	✦	598 blue (bks 435)	●	3781 dark brown

Patchwork Quilt

Cross stitched in a single colour and in a relatively large stitch, this doll's cradle quilt is simple to make – so simple that, with a little adult guidance, a young girl could easily embroider the design.
This is based on a traditional American patchwork pattern called Martha Washington's Star.

PATCHWORK QUILT

YOU WILL NEED

For a Doll's cradle quilt, measuring
41cm × 25cm (16in × 10in):

*46cm × 30cm (18in × 12in) of white linen,
20 threads to 2.5cm (1in)
43.5cm × 27.5cm (17in × 11in) of white linen,
finer than the above, or cotton backing fabric
43.5cm × 27.5cm (17in × 11in) of lightweight
synthetic batting
3 skeins of red 666 DMC stranded
embroidery cotton
No18 tapestry needle
Matching sewing thread*

●

THE EMBROIDERY

Stretch the prepared fabric in a frame, see page 5. Using three strands of thread in the needle and working one cross stitch over two threads of fabric, follow the chart to complete one half of the embroidery. Repeat, embroidering the second half as instructed on the chart.

When stitching, bear in mind that with very openweave fabrics it is better not to strand the embroidery thread from one area to another, since the thread will show through on the right side. Trim any long threads, and steam press the finished embroidery on the wrong side.

COMBINING THE LAYERS

Trim the top fabric to measure 43.5cm × 27.5cm (17in × 11in), and place it face down. Centre the batting on top and then lay the backing fabric over the batting, smoothing all layers as you go. Pin and baste the three layers together, stitching outward from the centre. In this way, by smoothing the fabrics out towards the edges, you will avoid unsightly puckering in the middle of the quilt. Baste horizontally, vertically and diagonally both ways. Baste from the centre outwards; leave a long tail at the centre and work out to one corner, then rethread the needle and work out to the other corner, avoiding knots at the centre.

TYING THE QUILT

Working on the right side, and using either matching sewing thread or quilting thread if you prefer, make a single stitch in the centre of each square that depicts a cross. Bring the needle out to the right side, leaving an 8cm (3in) tail underneath; make a tiny stitch in the centre of the cross, and return the needle to the wrong side. Make a second stitch at the same point. On the wrong side, tie the ends together – right over left, left over right – but do not pull too tightly. Trim the ends of the knot. Complete, tying all knots in this way.

FINISHING THE EDGES

Trim the batting by 12mm (½in) all around the edge. Turn under the seam allowances of the top and backing, bringing that of the top over the edge of the batting. Baste and then, using matching thread, slipstitch around the edges. For a traditional finish, hand quilt around the edge, setting the first row two threads in from the edge and the second row eight threads in, just clear of the embroidered border.

Remove the basting threads and lightly steam press if necessary.

HAND QUILTING

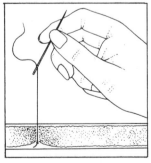 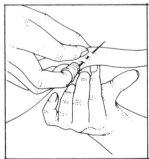

1 Working in a hoop will keep your fabric evenly stretched and give a pleasant puffed effect to the finished quilting. Using a quilting needle and a fairly short length of quilting thread, knot the end. Pull the knot through the backing fabric and into the batting.

2 With a thimble on the second finger of the sewing hand, make several stitches. Keep your

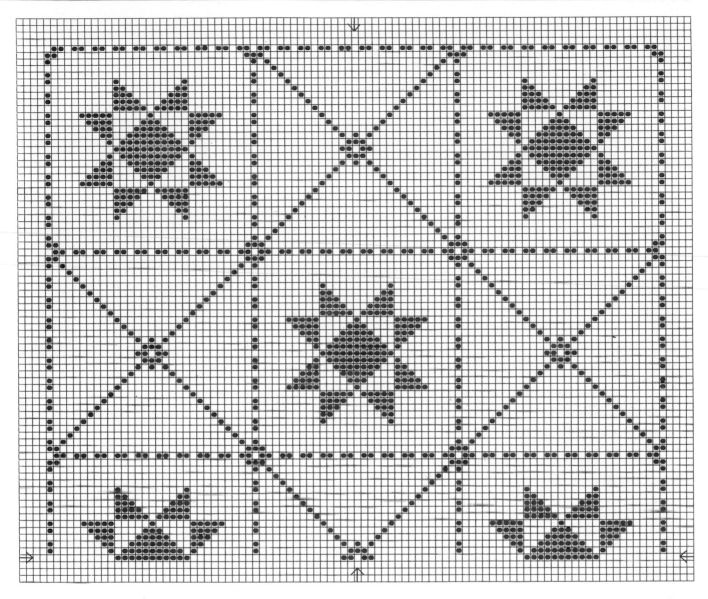

thumb pressed down on the fabric, just ahead of the needle, while the hand below, also with a thimble on the first or second finger, feels the needle and guides it back through the layers.

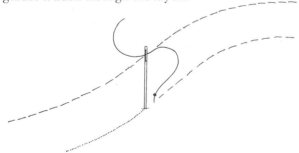

3 Finish off with a couple of back stitches or make a knot close to the last stitch and take the thread through to the back. Pull the knot through into the batting and cut the thread.

PATCHWORK QUILT ▲

● 666   red

Complete the second half of the design by embroidering in reverse from the centre line.

Scatter Cushions

Make this charming set of tiny
cushions to scatter on a young
teenager's bed, or mix them with other
cushions to fill an armchair or sofa.
The scale of these cushions is small,
but you could easily increase the size
by adding a border of velvet, in a dark
matching shade, effectively
framing the centres.

SCATTER CUSHIONS

YOU WILL NEED

For three cushion covers, each measuring
24cm (9½in) square:

*58cm × 29cm (23in × 11½in) each of cream,
pink and grey evenweave Aida fabric,
14 threads to 2.5cm (1in)
100cm (40in) each of gold (metallic), grey and red
fabric-covered piping
DMC stranded embroidery cotton in the colours
given in the appropriate panel
No24 tapestry needle
Matching sewing threads
Three 25cm (10in) square cushion pads
Tracing paper*

•

THE EMBROIDERY

All three cushions are made in the same way. To
make one cushion, cut the evenweave fabric in half
to give two pieces, each measuring 29cm (11½in)
square. Following the instructions given on page
5, prepare and stretch one of the pieces of fabric
in an embroidery frame.

Referring to the appropriate chart, and colour
key, complete the cross stitching, using two strands
of thread in the needle throughout, and working the
backstitch details on top. Finish by backstitching
the outline around the design, working each quarter
section symmetrically, and again, using two strands
of the thread in the needle.

Remove the embroidery from the frame and
steam press on the wrong side.

MAKING UP THE CUSHION COVER

Trim the edges of the embroidery and the backing
section of evenweave so that they each measure
26.5cm (10½in) square. Following the outline of
the cushion corner given with the chart for the Pied
Piper, make a template from tracing paper, rever-
sing each corner on the centre lines to complete the
cushion shape. Using the template, mark and then
cut around the curved corners on both sections of

evenweave fabric. A 12mm (½in) seam allowance
is included.

Metallic gold piping has been used for the
Rumplestiltskin design, red for the Pied Piper and
grey for The Goosegirl. Lay the piping on the right
side of the embroidery, placing the raw edge just
inside the seam allowance. Baste, and then use the
piping foot to machine stitch it in place (see page
6). Overlap the two ends, neatly angling the raw
edges into the seam allowance. If the piping can be
spliced (unlike purchased metallic varieties), this
would give an invisible join.

With right sides of the cushion front and back
together, baste and machine stitch around the
edges, leaving a 16cm (6¼in) opening in the
middle of one side, again using the piping foot, and
stitching as close as possible to the piping.

Remove the basting threads, snip into the
corners and turn the cover to the right side. Before
inserting the cushion pad, give the corners a
slightly rounded shape by tucking in the point of
each corner by about 12mm (½in). Finger-press
the resultant rounded shaping for about 4cm (1½in)
on each side of the point, gently easing the curve
into the side seams at each corner. Loosely overcast
the seam to hold the shape. Insert the cushion pad,
turn in the opening and slipstitch to close, using
matching sewing thread.

PIED PIPER ▶

↑   725 yellow
◣   741 amber
I   370 ochre (bks 317)
S   3779 flesh (bks 927)
✱   606 red (bks 317)
⊡   309 magenta (bks 317)
◹   703 green
○   943 veridian green (bks 317)
●   3052 drab green
◆   927 light grey (bks 317)
↓   317 grey (rat's feet; bks 927)
△   413 dark grey (all whiskers and
       piper's moustache)

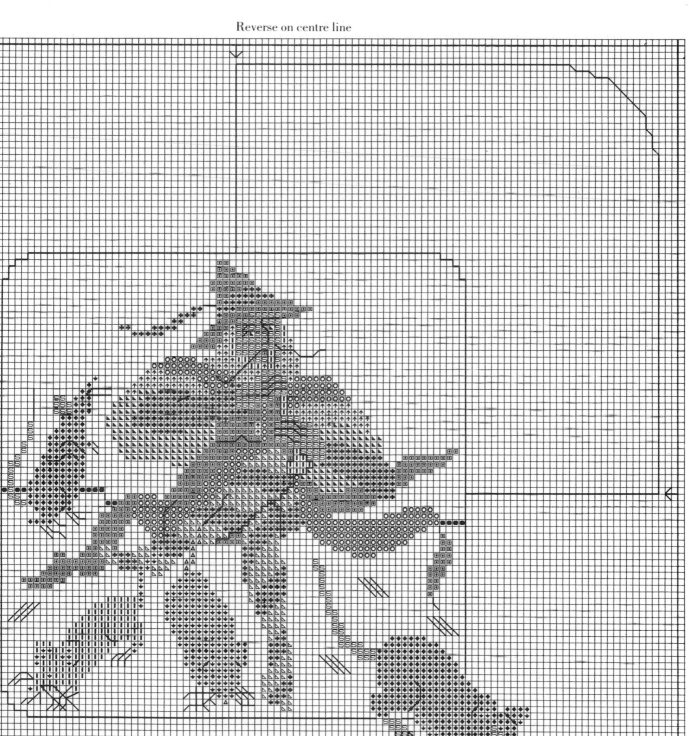

THE PIED PIPER

The Pied Piper put his brass flute to his lips and began to play a
sad, haunting melody. Suddenly, the streets of Hamelin seethed
with rats; the Pied Piper walked towards the river and sat down,
whereupon the rats threw themselves into the icy water and
disappeared forever.

THE GOOSEGIRL

The princess, tricked by her servant
into minding geese, speaks to the
head of her horse Falada. Every
morning, as she sets out to tend her
flock of geese, she stops at the
gateway and says, 'Alas, dear
Falada, there you hang.' And Falada
answers, 'Alas, Queen's daughter,
there you go, if your mother knew
your fate, her heart would break with
grief so great.' Then she goes on her
way till she comes to the common,
where she sits down and begins to
comb out her hair.

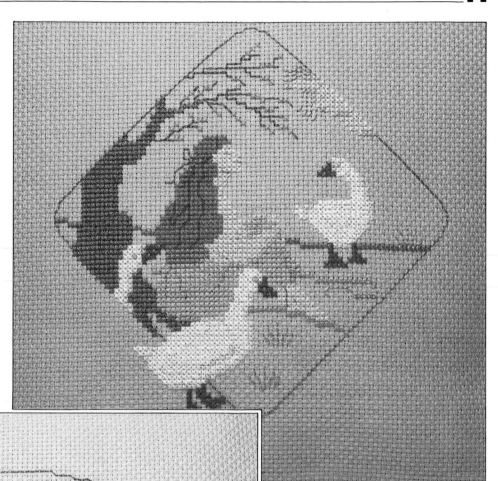

RUMPLESTILTSKIN

Appearing suddenly, as if from
nowhere, the rather eccentric and
diminutive little man asked the
miller's daughter, 'What will you
give me if I spin the straw into gold?'
'The ring from my finger', she
replied. Rumplestiltskin hopped
onto the stool and began to spin.
In just a few minutes he had changed
the pile of straw into a hundred
bobbins of pure gold thread.

RUMPLESTILTSKIN ▲

⊑	834 corn (and bks stems)
✦	725 yellow (bks 3045)
○	gold thread (and thread being spun; bks 3045)
◆	3779 flesh (bks 3011)
●	3712 red (bks 3766)
◣	3753 pale turquoise (bks 3766)
⊡	3766 turquoise (bks 3347)
		3347 green
△	3045 light brown (bks 3011)
✳	3011 brown (bks 3045)

THE GOOSEGIRL ▼

=   white (bks 3072)
◆   725 yellow (bks 3013)
↑   834 gold (bks 725)
| 948 flesh (bks 3706;
           bks eye 927)
●   3354 dusky pink (bks outline
           around design)
◁   3706 deep pink (bks hair ribbon)

○   927 drab turquoise (bks 3354)
∽   772 pale green (bks grass)
↓   3013 olive green
⊡   3052 drab green (bks tree
           branches)
△   3072 grey (bks 927 on sleeve;
           bks 926 on horse)
✱   926 dark grey

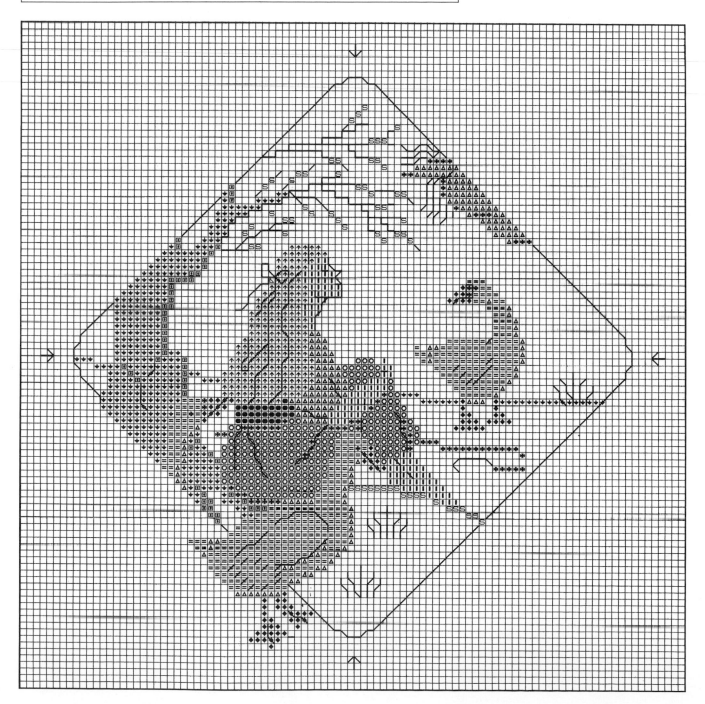

With Love and Kisses

What better way to send a special greeting than with a card you've made yourself? Choose doves and hearts to celebrate a new baby's arrival or christening, jolly Santa Claus for Christmas, or two colourful parrots for a toddler's second birthday.

Each motif is easily stitched, and displayed in a press-together card mount which couldn't be quicker or simpler to use.

WITH LOVE
AND KISSES

YOU WILL NEED

For the Christening card, measuring overall 20cm × 14.5cm (8in × 5¾in), with a rectangular portrait cut out, 14cm × 9.5cm (5½in × 3¼in):

23cm × 18cm (9in × 7¼in) of pale pink linen, 28 threads to 2.5cm (1in)
DMC stranded embroidery cotton in the colours given in the appropriate panel
No26 tapestry needle
Best Wishes greetings card mount (for suppliers, see page 2)

For the Santa Claus christmas greetings card, measuring overall 14cm × 9cm (5½in × 3½in), with an oval cut out, 9cm × 7cm (3½in × 2¾in):

17cm × 13cm (6¾in × 5in) of pale green linen, 28 threads to 2.5cm (1in)
DMC stranded embroidery cotton in the colours given in the appropriate panel
No26 tapestry needle
Christmas card mount (for suppliers, see page 2)

For the Second birthday card, measuring overall 20cm × 14.5cm (8in × 5¾in), with a rectangular portrait cut out, 14cm × 9.5cm (5½in × 3¾in):

23cm × 18cm (9in × 7¼in) of white evenweave Aida fabric, 18 thread to 2.5cm (1in)
DMC stranded embroidery cotton in the colours given in the appropriate panel
No26 tapestry needle
Birthday greetings card mount (for suppliers, see page 2)

•

THE EMBROIDERY

Prepare the fabric and mount it in a small hoop, following the instructions on page 4. When embroidering greetings cards, it is important to avoid too much overstitching on the back of the fabric in order to prevent unsightly lumps showing on the right side. For the Santa Claus and Christen-ing designs, work one cross stitch over two threads of fabric throughout.

Referring to the appropriate chart and colour key, complete the cross stitching, using two strands of thread in the needle for all three designs. You will find it easier to embroider Santa's beard if you stitch the pale grey shadows first, and then fill in with white. Similarly, complete the motif first on the cradle of the Christening design before filling in with white. Steam press the embroidery on the wrong side.

CHRISTENING CARD ▼		
⊡ 734 green (and bks border)		
I white	○ 828 pale blue	
✱ silver, plus bks around doves	△ 3072 pale grey	
◆ 725 ochre		
● 957 pink		

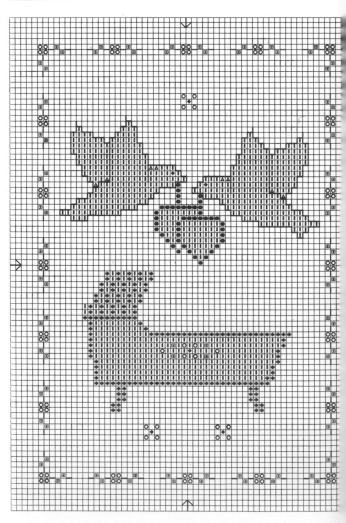

If you leave the basting stitches in at this stage, you will find them useful in helping to centre your design on the card.

ASSEMBLING THE CARDS

Open out the three sections of the card. Trim the embroidery until it is about 12mm (½in) larger than the marked area around the cut-out window. Using the basting stitches as a guide, centre the motif over the cut-out area — measuring an equal distance at each side of the basting — and press in place.

Remove the basting stitches. Fold over the left-hand section of the card and press to cover the embroidery, giving a neat permanent seal to your special greetings card.

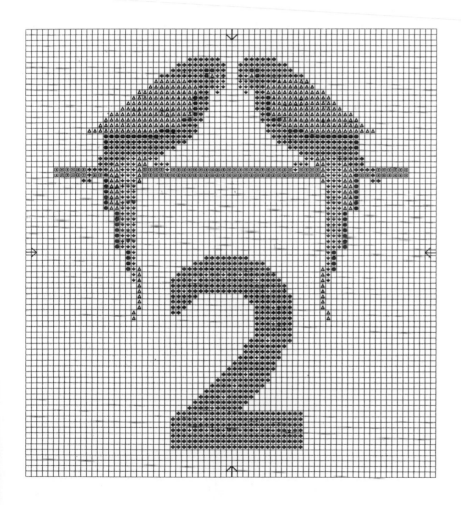

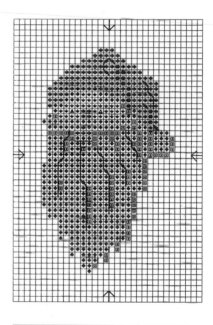

SANTA CLAUS ▲

◆   white
↓   754   flesh
✖   606   red
●   347   dark red
      (and bks hat)
△   518   blue
⊡   3072   pale grey
      (and bks beard)

SECOND BIRTHDAY ▲

↓   725   yellow
✖   351   red
△   704   green
⊡   734   olive green
●   798   blue

Frilled Baby Basket

This pretty and practical basket,
designed to hold all baby's odds and
ends, would delight any new mother.
The tie-on washable cover can easily
be removed for laundering – and when
baby grows up you can always use the
basket for toys or for family shopping.
The cover is designed for a basket
with a top measuring approximately
29cm × 42cm (11½in × 16½in),
but the size can easily
be adjusted.
The design could also be adapted to a
Moses basket, but in this case, having
measured the basket and made an
allowance for the baby's head, it
would be best to cut the fabric straight
across at the head end, and take the
frill around the sides and bottom only.
You could also cut the back and
batting in one piece and omit the ties,
so that the top will fit snugly
around the baby.

FRILLED BABY-BASKET COVER

YOU WILL NEED

For a cover measuring approximately
33cm × 46cm (13in × 18in) across, including a
3cm (1¼in) frill all around:

*33cm × 46cm (13in × 18in) of white evenweave
Linda fabric, or linen, 16 threads to 2.5cm (1in)
33cm × 46cm (13in × 18in) of white cotton lawn
for the lining
28cm × 40cm (11in × 16in) of medium-weight
synthetic batting
160cm (1¾yd) of white pre-gathered broderie
anglaise edging, 4cm (1½in) wide
140cm (1½yd) of white taffeta ribbon,
2.5cm (1in) wide
DMC stranded embroidery cotton in the colours
given in the panels
Matching sewing threads
Baby basket of your choice
Tracing paper*

●

PREPARING THE FABRIC

First, enlarge the graph pattern on to tracing paper
(see page 6); mark the positioning lines for the
embroidery, and cut out.

Baste the centre of the embroidery fabric both
ways; place the paper pattern on the straight grain,
matching the centre lines, and baste around the
curved edge. Repeat on the opposite side. Mark the
positioning lines for the two motifs, as shown on the
graph pattern.

Using the paper pattern, cut out the batting and
the lining fabric, adding a 12mm (½in) seam allowance all around on the lining pieces, and around
the curved edge only on the batting sections.

THE EMBROIDERY

With the prepared fabric stretched in a hoop, begin
the embroidery. Following the charts given opposite, and working with two strands of thread in the
needle, complete the cross stitching. Finish by
working the backstitch details, using a single
strand of thread.

Steam press on the wrong side. Cut out, adding
a 12mm (½in) seam allowance all round.

MAKING THE COVER

Working on the right side, baste the lace edging
around the outer edge of the embroidered section,
with the raw edge placed just inside the seam allowance, and leaving a 3cm (1¼in) space in the
middle of both long sides. This will allow the cover
to fit snugly around the basket handle, and the two
sides to be lifted independantly. Turn under the
short edges of the frill twice to neaten.

With the embroidery and the two lining sections
right sides together, place the batting on top. Baste
and machine stitch around the outer edge. Trim the
batting close to the seam, clip into the curves and
turn the cover through to the right side. Turn under
the two straight edges of the lining, unpicking a few
stiches of the outer seam as necessary, then baste
and machine stitch across.

Cut the ribbon in half and attach to each side,
stitching the centre of the ribbon over the seam
allowance in the space left, to neaten. Remove all
basting threads and lightly press to finish.

BABY BASKET COVER

1 SQUARE = 2.5cm (1in)

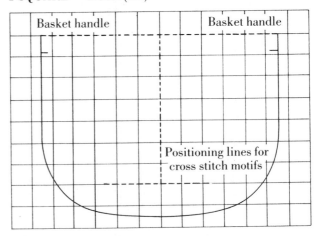

CUT TWO FROM BATTING
CUT TWO FROM LINING
Reverse on centre line and cut
one for cover top

◀ SWALLOW

◆ 3047 cream

◣ 3078 pale yellow
     (bks 725)

↓ 725 yellow (bks 798)

○ 745 flesh (eyes 798,
     mouth 350)

⊡ 602 deep pink (bks 336)

✳ 350 vermilion

I 798 pale blue (bks 824)

△ 824 blue

● 336 dark blue

BUTTERFLY ▶

○ 3078 pale yellow
     (bks inner
     veins 725)

◆ 725 yellow
     (bks 350)

⊡ 602 deep pink

✳ 350 vermilion

↓ 3747 pale blue

● 824 blue
     (bks antennae)

△ 676 deep buff
     (bks 350)

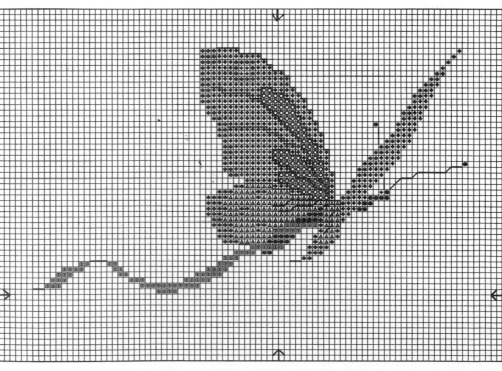

Miniature Pictures

What better way to build up a pretty collection of pictures than to embroider them yourself?

Taken from three nursery rhymes – 'Little maid, pretty maid, whither goest thou?', 'Rock-a-bye, baby, on the tree top', and 'A little girl quite well and hearty', any of these small pictures would make a lovely gift for a child and – who knows? – might perhaps encourage the child to take up embroidery herself.

If you decide to embroider all three designs, it would obviously be preferable to use the same background colour for each. The little girl and the sleeping baby would both look attractive against the blue background.

If you prefer to keep to a cream fabric, it might be a good idea to backstitch in grey around the mob cap and along the edge of the apron where the white would meet the cream.

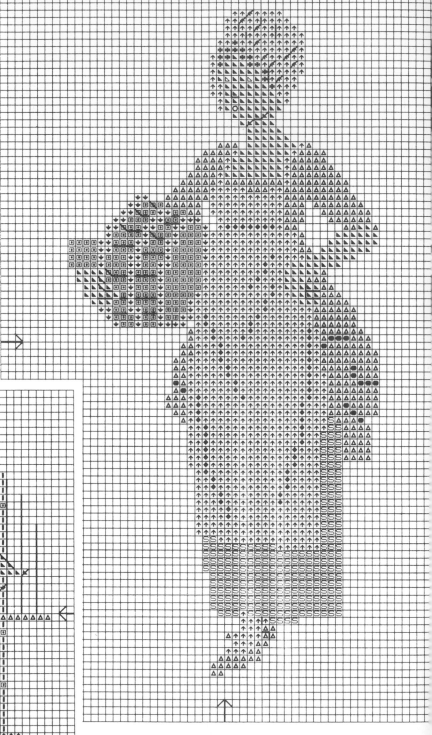

QUITE WELL, QUITE HEARTY ▼

- ○ 963 pink (bks 335, initial M 3041)
- ⊡ 335 deep pink (bks 3041)
- ↓ 948 flesh
- ✱ 3041 purple (bks 3011)
- ‖ 966 green
- ◆ 3052 sap green
- ◣ 307 yellow (eye 833)
- △ 833 ochre (bks cage, bird's legs)
- ● 3011 dark brown

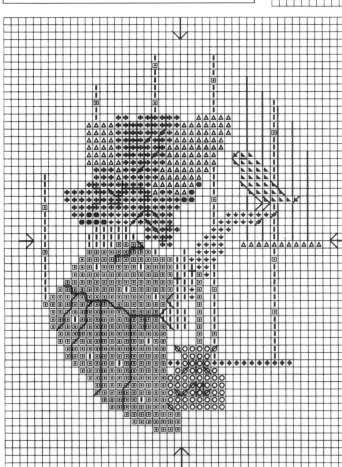

LITTLE MAID ◀

- ↑ white (and bks 318*)
- ◣ 948 flesh (bks 352)
- ○ 352 pink
- △ 800 blue
- ● 823 navy blue
- △ 312 dark blue
- ⊡ 436 light brown (bks 434)
- ✱ 434 brown
- ◆ 415 pale grey
- ↓ 648 grey

Note: one additional backstitch colour*

ROCK-A-BYE BABY ▼

- = white
- ↑ 726 yellow
- | 676 gold
- ◣ 754 flesh
  (bks eye 3688)
- △ 3688 pink
- ● 602 deep pink
- △ 3756 pale blue
  green (bks 519)
- ⊡ 519 blue green
- ∽ 955 pale green
- ↓ 913 green (bks twigs)
- ◆ 951 fawn
- ✱ 3011 brown

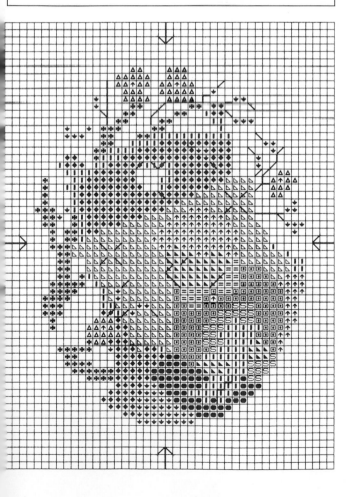

MINIATURE PICTURES

YOU WILL NEED

For the *Little Maid* picture, measuring
18cm × 13cm (7¼in × 5in):

*23cm × 18cm (9in × 7¼in) of blue evenweave
(Aida) fabric, 18 threads to 2.5cm (1in)
DMC stranded embroidery cotton in the colours
given in the appropriate panel
No 26 tapestry needle
Oval brass frame (for suppliers, see page 2)*

For *Quite Well, Quite Hearty,* and
Rock-a-Bye Baby miniatures, each measuring
11.5cm × 9cm (4½in × 3½in):

*28cm × 18cm (11in × 7¼in) of white evenweave
linen, 26 threads to 2.5 cm (1in)
DMC stranded embroidery cotton in the colours
given in the appropriate panels
No 26 tapestry needle
Two oval brass frames (for suppliers, see page 2)*

•

THE EMBROIDERY

Each picture is worked in the following way. With the prepared fabric stretched in a hoop and the centre marked both ways, see page 4, you are ready to begin the cross stitching. Use two strands of thread in the needle throughout, except for the backstitching of *Little Maid*, which is worked in a single strand. When working a fairly openweave fabric, such as the linen used here, bear in mind that threads should not be stranded across an open area or they will be seen from the right side.

Remove the fabric from the frame and steam press on the wrong side, if necessary.

MAKING UP THE PICTURES

Follow the manufacturer's instructions for assembling the pictures, checking that you have allowed sufficient fabric to fill the frame before cutting out by fitting the paper template supplied into the frame.

Tied-on Pillow Cover

Dress up a plain yellow pillow with
this pretty tied-on cover, embroidered
on crisp white evenweave cotton.
The idea is practical as well as pretty,
for the embroidered cover can easily
be removed at night-time, to cut
down on laundering.

The little boy blue of the nursery
rhyme, incidentally, is an allusion to
Cardinal Wolsey, who neglected his
flock in his attempts to engineer the
divorce of Henry VIII.

TIED-ON PILLOW COVER

YOU WILL NEED

For a pillow cover measuring 46cm × 35cm (18in × 14in):

48.5cm × 38cm (19in × 15in) of white evenweave (Aida) fabric, 14 threads to 2.5cm (1in)
48.5cm × 38cm (19in × 15in) of white backing fabric, either fine cotton or linen
250cm (2⅔yds) of cornflower blue satin ribbon, 2cm (¾in) wide
140cm (1½yds) of cornflower blue bias binding
DMC stranded embroidery cotton in the colours given in the panel
No24 tapestry needle
Matching sewing thread

•

THE EMBROIDERY

With the prepared fabric stretched in a frame, see page 5, baste the positioning lines for the motif, following the chart given opposite.

Using two strands of thread in the needle throughout, work all the cross stitching first and then the backstitching.

Take out the basting stitches; remove the fabric from the frame, and steam press on the wrong side.

MAKING UP THE PILLOW COVER

With right sides together, baste the top and backing fabric along the two long edges. Machine stitch, taking 12mm (½in) seams. Press the seams open.

For the ties, cut the ribbon into eight equal lengths. With the wrong side facing, baste them in pairs to each of the short edges, placing them 10cm (4in) in from the corners (see the diagram below).

Cover the short edges with bias binding, at the same time enclosing the ribbon ends. Overlap the raw edges of the binding at the seams. Press and turn through to the right side. Slip the cover over a contrast pillow and tie in place.

LITTLE BOY BLUE ▶

◹ white (bks 341)
ॼ 744 yellow (bks 738)
↓ 738 corn
◆ 834 deep yellow
I 3779 flesh (bks 3712)
△ 3712 red (bks 3052)
○ 341 blue (bks 792)
● 792 dark blue (bks eye; bks 3011)
✳ 3052 olive
⊡ 3011 brown

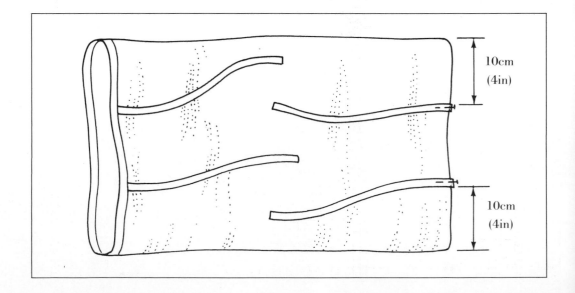

10cm (4in)

10cm (4in)

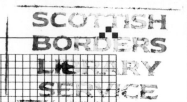

ACKNOWLEDGEMENTS

The author would like to offer her grateful thanks to the
following people who helped with the cross stitching of
projects in this book with such skill and enthusiasm:
Clarice Blakey, Caroline Davies, Christina Eustace,
Janet Grey, and to Julie Hasler for her design
Little Maid on page 40.
Thanks are also due to DMC Creative World Ltd
for providing the black and white charts.

CONVERSION CHART

Not all of these colour conversions are exact matches, and bracketed
numbers are given as close substitutes.

DMC	ANCHOR	COATS	MADEIRA	DMC	ANCHOR	COATS	MADEIRA	DMC	ANCHOR	COATS	MADEIRA
White	2	1001	White	606	335	2334	0209	926	(779)	6007	1707
224	893	3241	0813	611	898	—	2107	927	(849)	6006	1708
307	(289)	2290	0104	648	900	8390	1814	943	188	—	1203
309	(42)	3284	0507	666	46	3046	0210	948	(778)	2331	0306
312	(147)	7979	1005	676	891	2305	2208	951	(880)	—	2308
317	(400)	8512	1714	703	238	6238	1307	955	203	—	1210
334	161	7977	1003	704	(256)	6238	1308	957	52	—	0612
336	149	—	1007	725	(306)	2298	0108	963	48	—	0608
341	117	—	0901	726	295	2294	0109	966	206	—	1209
347	(19)	3013	0407	733	280	—	1611	3011	856	—	1607
350	(11)	3011	0213	734	(279)	—	1610	3041	871	—	0806
351	(10)	3012	0214	738	942	5375	2013	3045	(888)	—	2103
352	(9)	3008	0303	741	304	2314	0201	3047	(886)	2300	2205
370	(888)	—	2112	744	(301)	2293	0112	3052	(844)	—	1509
413	401	8514	1713	745	(300)	2296	0111	3072	847	—	1805
415	398	8510	1803	754	(6)	2331	0305	3078	292	2292	0102
434	309	5000	2009	772	(264)	6250	1604	3347	(267)	6266	1408
435	(365)	5371	2010	783	307	—	2211	3688	(66)	—	0605
436	(363)	5943	2011	792	941	7150	0905	3705	(35)	—	0410
453	(869)	—	1806	798	(131)	7022	0911	3706	(33)	—	0409
504	213	—	1701	800	(128)	—	0908	3712	10	—	—
518	162	—	1106	807	(168)	—	1109	3733	75	—	—
519	167	—	1514	823	150	—	1008	3747	120	—	—
523	(215)	—	1512	824	(164)	—	1010	3753	(975)	—	—
581	(280)	—	1609	828	(158)	—	1101	3756	158	—	—
597	(168)	—	1110	833	907	—	2114	3766	167	—	—
598	(928)	—	1111	834	874	—	2204	3779	4146	—	—
602	(63)	3063	0702	913	(921)	7051	1711	3781	(905)	—	—